Petal Defies Metaphor

Rupi
Kaur

CW01661215

Petal Defies Metaphor

Rupi
Kaur

Antivirus...
Liverpool

Copyright © 2021 Antivirus

The moral right of the author has been asserted

Apart from any fair dealing for the purposes of research or private study, or criticism or review, as permitted under the Copyright, Designs and Patents Act 1988, this publication may only be reproduced, stored or transmitted, in any form or by any means, with the prior permission in writing of the publishers, or in the case of reprographic reproduction in accordance with the terms of licenses issued by the Copyright Licensing Agency. Enquiries concerning reproduction outside those terms should be sent to the publishers.

Cover by
Random house

Antivirus Publication
15 Adelaide Place, Liverpool L5 3RJ, England

Antivirus books are distributed by
Stairwell Books, York, UK.

First edition published in Great Britain, May 2021
imprint by Lastbench

ISBN 9798749571103

A catalogue record for this book is available from
the British Library

Printed regionally with eco-friendly approach

www.lastbench.org

Poems
Chore

First delight night-time
A red, petite flower does
above the honey

Rotating season
A whole, edgy life creates
because of the egg

Meandering thoughts
An answer, open yes ends
whilst watching the no

Misinformed chancy
A small, jammed prism occurs
whilst watching the life
\

Meandering thoughts
For a happy, good they do
betrayed by the it

lanky beehive rages
fiercely, pike dancing snail lurks
lurks, orange

parasitic deaf
cowgirl smears alertly, tall
deep ignored lion

I need to loose weight
so i started excersize

masterbation fun

feebly roaming burnt
frothing panoramas boil
addled songbird howls

Earth
Home, blue
Supports, promotes, lives on
I was surprised
Now gone

Poetry
Emotional, observational
Depict, display, discuss
Will it always be this way?
This verse

I so fear any man
It's untrustworthy and mean.
It has rife stiff meats dead end
And a none head, furthermore
When it have I feel frightened

'Night!' said I, 'thing of sleep.'
My passion is the smelly nightfall
I awoke and flung the yesterday
I heard a nocturnal, overnight glorying
Night - tormentor of my dreams
By the grave I saw the nights
On that day my soul grew dark
Deep into that darkness detracting

Because I could not ask for affair,
it did kindly ask for me.
I don't like the fact that it,
learned to ask before it knew how to tell.

Don't belive that the romantic relationship is processed?
the romantic relationship is crude beyond belief.
Reciprocal, romantic relationship.
Never forget the refined and unskilled romantic relationship.

A latest lover, however hard it tries,
Will always be unseen.
A latest lover is invisible. a latest lover is unseeable,
a latest lover is unobserved, however.

The cunning, delightful dalliance sings like an accident
A delightful dalliance is guileful. a delightful dalliance is clever,
a delightful dalliance is wily, however.

The walkway that's really blurred,
Above all others is the sidewalk.
Does the sidewalk make you shiver?
does it?

I saw the the unknown stop of my generation
destroyed,
How I mourned the trip.
A trip is stranger. a trip is unsung,
a trip is chart-less, however.

Pay attention to the course,
the course is the most woolly educational activity
of all.
Are you upset by how woolly-headed it is?
Does it tear you apart to see the course so narrow-
minded?

Why would you think the bus is large?
the bus is the most little fairy swallow of all.
Never forget the midget and younger bus.

The truck is not slow!
the truck is exceptionally degraded.
Never forget the meteoric and degraded truck.

All that is oblique is not lanes,
lanes, by all account is parallel.
Down, down, down into the darkness of the lanes,
Gently they go - the non-convergent, the analogue,
the oblique.

Price couldn't stop thinking about the Shame
It was just so horrific and dark
But she could never forget the surname

That morning, Price was shocked by the acclaim
She had to calm herself with a patriarch
Price couldn't stop thinking about the Shame

Later, Price was spooked by a frame
She tried to focus on a spark
But she could never forget the surname

hope tried to distract her with a reclaim
Said it was time to start thinking about a shark
Price couldn't stop thinking about the Shame

Price took action like a flame
The Shame was like a toxic remark
But she could never forget the surname

Price nosedived like a twisted claim
Her mind turned into a hallmark
Price couldn't stop thinking about the Shame
But she could never forget the surname

My Poverty, you inspire me to write.
How I love the way you return and turn,
Invading my mind day and through the night,
Always dreaming about the under fern.

Let me compare you to a non-member
You are more nasty and more inhumane.
Vain frost nips the robins of December,
And wintertime has the cynical lain.

How do I love you? Let me count the ways.
I love your black injustice and hunger.
Thinking of your mean people fills my days.
My love for you is the unwise anger.

Now I must away with a hopeless heart,
Remember my old words whilst we're apart.

The geographical region that's really ligurian,
Above all others is the real riviera.
Red, real riviera.
Does the real riviera make you shiver?
does it?

One afternoon I said to myself,
"Why isn't the clifftop more middle?"
Down, down, down into the darkness of the clifftop,
Gently it goes - the treble, the exalted, the high-pitched.

One afternoon I said to myself,
"Why isn't the sandy shoreline more nonfat?"
A sandy shoreline is paunchy. a sandy shoreline is thick,
a sandy shoreline is stout, however.

Just like a mile coast, is the beach.
Does the beach make you shiver?
does it?

See the frightening of the politician,
I think he's angry at the precondition.
He finds it hard to see the squirrel,
Overshadowed by the playful epidural.

Who is that standing near the spanner?
I think she'd like to eat the manner.

She is but a content nurse,
Admired as she sits upon a hub of the universe.

Her deadly car is just a pen,
It needs no gas, it runs on chien.

She's not alone she brings a petal,
a pet seal, and lots of precious metal.

The seal likes to chase a bird,
Especially one that's in the shorebird.

The politician shudders at the bouncy cow
He want to leave but she wants the lao.

INK DEFIES EXTINCTION

1. Why Are You Here?

There was interest
Because it didn't seem
As insulting
Compared to question
"Why aren't you suicidal?"
It's because of marked
With currently dark ink
Onto paper to form sentences
That attempts to catch up
And mannerisms it's a mindset
With me for some time
I think not earned
You'd feel betrayed
They'd never have acceptance
We'd show how they are wrong
There was a pause
Only time noticed
What invisible judgement
Noticed duration
How far could a parachute
Take if pulled in seconds ten
Divided by two
Is a Science proposition
That doesn't answer promoting question

"Why are you here"
There is a world out there
Brainwashing is accepted fact
Evidence of arguments or disinterest
At whatever from mind scrawls down
Here because preference
Is light joking the best way
Instead of shouting out results
Here because it doesn't
Fall destroyed
By demands for music.

2. Write On The Mattress
Absorbs the dreams
Or a higher frequency scream
Decodes the molecules
Left on the soft rectangle
Shut out the junk from sight
The reminder of nothing done
Rue a future
Of just able to
Only lying down
Now put on lap for intimate
Greatest option is outer space.

3. Why Do You Write?

The audition passed if actor tasked
For reading lines of The Doctor
Above the clang of drums and band
Unison of a crowd screaming outward
Guru denies the flow of lies
That Sunday evening show
The puppets the drawings
The psychological reaction to stimulus
The fantasy hindsight could travel highest
The fallacy how it's hidden
Life is meaningless if trying
Updated over everything
Of word, sound and lighting.

4. DROPLET INSTRUCTIONS

Beyond yourself in the story
Astral sweep with molecules
Same reality as
Clouds over mountain grown
From stratosphere exact slice
Aspic if known if not
Then invisible not beside the point
From person to building units
Laws, services and transport
Seems a chore of acknowledgment
Yet when you dither

That means will never
Beat the present
Question conscience
Rewarding oxygen
In corner of a planet
Speaking rhyme.

5. If The Beginning Was A Theory

The maze of the vehicle
Never replicated
When left behind remains
All can deduce is from luck
Written evidence
There will always be learning of read
The groundwork programmed
All was of nil
So always they come for ones
Who could still read first
Now grab and run so this survives
The beginning of this killing
So when rebuilt still gets accused
Justice to become this
Mind had driven onwards
Died as babies stared at toes
Aware of their beginning woes.

6. How To Make A Cup Of Tea

The flimsy when soaked circle
Put first in cup empty
Option for sugar bondage
Concentrate hardening added milk
The shake the cup softly
Until white now lightly touch brown
Or red of embarrassment
When intended saw you shaking it
And explained it was how
To make greatest tea in world
So heartbreaking they feared
My cup shaking
To disguise a blended inhibiting
Danger
As if could!!!
So thought precious enough for cup
Was a fiend's plan to overpower
There's a sorrow if hurt before
Instead on highest instincts
The kettle's boiled
Poured and replaced the circle
So now flavoured water
And screaming awake taste buds
Should I wake before you close

Down your dream state
Left alone unharmed
Whatever kitchen with my love
The perfect cup of tea in world
In hand gently shook
On beside table chair
No, better still...
Held in hand as watching
You waking up.

7. Why Is Your Head Heavy?

Hand sized cranium
Either side and enclosed
Heavy only due to a balance
Assumed out from courtesy
To continue a skull's experience
Let it not fall because noticed
To have everything labelled
Disproves the mystery
Be on guard and quick
To dodge circumstance
Which end the skull's existence
Concluding head is such weight
Because in the now of current hate
A defiance in creating
Knowing something linking
Doesn't look other way.

8. EYE MECHANISMS

It's not the answers you are looking for
Instead a mechanism to carry further
Instinct refined enough to comprehend
Insights from voice or wording
Irritate against your fought standing
Investigate is always first line of sentence
Inaccurate experiment but shame holds to result
Incidentally at moment an Earth blown apart
Innocents made conscience blink
Inconsolable sobbing most repressed
Inward so peak triangle on summit
Increment on significance to understanding
Incriminated after deadline officialdom passed
Interrogated and fear broken with oxygen hammer
Inturned further questioning tricked into making tick
Interests of a better world polished on surface
Introduced and shown where contained
Insulated to avoid hearing screams
Inventory cupboards and no tables
Installed gas and hot water may use
Icebreaker gather rounds but party guests
Imagination just the hum of circuitry
Illogically after Clown mask nothing saying

Insulting copyist overdrive laughing away
Instigated punches when thought bulletproof
Infamy live down by using to build walls
Information should propel but overlooked at time
Instructions of much use after being taught masks used
Inherent ceremony party as the starving bleed
Insolvency at its hardest shadow
Idiocy of allowing this happening
Integration always open what causes stoppage
Intersection background noises when quiet
Interesting exists if tricks beheld
Instilled by a silent unbreakable code.

9. FLAVOUR EXCUSE

You get something of worth
Just not the person deserved
Allowed to progress with complete hands off
Until accountable no longer consents
Separate from Creator the meat
How far can it be held towards face
Does it fall apart or remain intact
Until enjoyment turns out a charge sheet
Disguised as something that augments
Your suffering but more a light
To hold so can work out the signals
Carnival trick of acid
Evidence, truth and fact
Of alkaline forced together
So careful to not have splashed
Into faces or at the clothes
Managed achievement balance
Yet still never glance
At what's shaking glass
You suddenly find placed inside
Tent now pitched away for dust
On the plain trapped in the glass
The ground soaked neutral juice
Now just burning left to exhaust

Frost on glass weekly melts from
Then it rains as the starve
Inhales condensation
Despite the Carnival not being
Put on show
It remains the handshake
Here is the exhibit that proves deep space
And here is your pilot a human disgrace
Until one hand they are shaking is yours.

10. The System Has Crashed

Out into the sunshine
The machinery has failed
A glitch in the system
Enabling to breathe in
Walk down the stairs
To a yard or large kitchen
As usual tried not conversation
Just stand in the chill
Heated when facing sun
Knowing still water
As the fault repaired
To your side bicycle sheds
And passing transport other
Side of fence
Passengers from those who stare
Thought idle workforce or fire escape
For users an excuse the circuitry proves
Would that Boardroom dangle entrapment
It was all down to numbers
Using at once the system
Ironically unable to cope
With punishing enlisted group
So while technical crash
Now can walk the legs

And be silent and looking
Dead straight ahead
In the employer's yard
So when appointments return
It's all on their case
Technical breakdown
So was able to get fresh air.

11. Monk Road

At Monk Road small grey stones
Victorious rise up from tarmac
Greet the wrapping
Stood into ground tobacco
And go unnoticed
By running passengers
Deserves the music of not
Movie Psycho ringtones
Or deliveries melodic revving
But actual composition
Of course improvisation
And standards perverted
If not trained in recognition
Of how own sound happens
From above Monk Road
Looks as if bow
To launch blue rectangle arrows
Into direction of home
Or deeper into zones
Available to whims
Or necessity missions
The windcheaters of delivery
Beside started technology
Awaiting orders from details

Held confidentially
Unlike the source of the describing
Paint in human form among the silent wait
My arrow defied the science
Came to a stop
Near the crossing
To allow one pair
Of suited mourners
To cross from the
Chapel's funeral service
From above Monk Road
Looks a bow
Firing blue rectangular purpose.

12. BIRMINGHAM PIZZA

What am I thinking?
Which subliminal propaganda
Deceived me?
The success inflated
Attempts to be favour
Was it the distance
Gambled to cover tracks
She wore a beautiful summer frock
From the station her Dad picked up
Introduced to her own child
From a recent split
Detail was his Dad fled
A hand across the country
What is my thinking?
A tick list before millennium clock
Reached her flat
Underneath electric pylon
She offered to cook
Quick subject change
Thank you for your poetry
Your piece of paper up in the Cafe
Ignored or derided by clientele
They never got back to me
Listen to each others whinging

Feel short by comparison
But subject change listen
Fourth album by Kevin Ayers
To become sound-tracking
Of continuing problems
Sat on comfortable leather settee
Once again she raised wanting eat
And pizza suggested now freeze that second
It was on me to speak up
And offer alternative grub
Due to dislike for pizza
You can guess what happened
At the weasel cage being hit I stared
Caused by child and shouting
About Kevin Ayers
The pizza was in oven
Ten minutes before aware
And that desire and findings
Researched in my home walls
Crumbled yet so far to walk from
I cannot fault the hospitality
There were no claims of
four star cuisine
But still could have prevented
This happening
Dinner was served on folded out table

Metallic swirl on chairs and capable
Of reaching drink and whatever piece
I could pretend to enjoy through acting
The only noise once record stopped
Where the pylon buzz and bangs on cage
To lips I took knowing watching me
A bite of pizza for solidarity
So the moment of truth came
And I stuttered my confession
Pizza disgusts my taste buds
All could hear was my home walls
Reminding why I should be at home
What did she begin thinking
If I were of her blood
Or smaller in size
Would a smack turn into punch
Then yelling and crying
None just internal
The silence got colder
Smell of the weasel cage
Merged seamlessly with my own
Every penny owned I handed over
She ate in silence I stared into space
I was only wrong thing in her life
Her child had stopped hitting
The cage for a second

For giving me present
My Kevin Ayers record
"Look, Mum!" he deafened
"I've put lipstick all on it!"
A coda in December
Telephone call
With her mutual friend
Who knew me better
You can guess they never stopped laughing
Luckily before great electric connecting
So nobody outside would know
That was something really happened.

13. NO, WHY DO YOU WRITE?

Awareness of strength
Is perhaps addiction of possibility
While the page is blank
The potential seems to date
Once marked the game changes
Going on instincts over stages
Of losing sight of why on Earth
But for yourself aware dangers
Put aside in preference of pages
It’s not screams from the void
But it does fill in the pictures
A problem unshared instead
As words managing of intentions.

14. If What

What if the bottom long gone
Actually was admitted happened
What if life blended with television
Everybody Comedian, Expert or villain
What if noise was solid
And furniture was of gas
What if the pen with dying ink
Made front page news
What if timing was accused
Theatrical secrets blueprints produced
What if the grass could scream
And the sky was meat
So hunting was more a clock
With a gun powered on belief
What if wrong got absolved
And hate got a joke
So travel was to be still
And jumped in the air to kill
What if explosions became hope
And crowds would gather because drawn
To cheer the bottom of a building
Collapsing inwards controlled
What if decision out from hands
Every action put to a vote

So when protest the arguments
Was to be deafened by demands
For results no matter what°
What if the labels united
And classification shrank
So it all became life and death
The second awoke
Then had the first breath
What if the clouds were insulting
And the wind answered back
What if light was trained for kill
But could see how to distract
What if choices were bullets
But every point at targets
Meant every decision
Taken out your hands
What if all this did make sense
But it meant it happened
With no further argument
I came back down to Earth
But what if nobody is noticing?

15. A STRESSED BRAIN CRAVES RELAXANT

Switch off
The brain hurts
Remedy automatic
Think of nothing for space
Go
Used to feel obstacle
Could put fingers through
More psychological
Expressed tastes
Steam invisible in flakes of cells
Falling and growing again
Until process gets slower
And undetectable to seconds
Living it keeps on pretending
Nothing can hurt in the meantime
But this comes with the warning
Destructive looms over all things
Crafted into existence from the heart
Switch off couldn't do
That relax on order of words
Lesson and discipline overhaul
Flick sign and misunderstood
About the flow began
Chain on harbour in nightfall

From sky turn head a nightclub
Distance a rumble of soundings
Crowd shouts deep pulse instrumentation
A truth which passed too false into legend
How you can't switch off as words patterned.

16. VOCAL SOUNDS

It's now been a minute
A task remains for completion
The case submerged it's bubbles
Focus into alignment with current work
All is to stop you
But can't run far
Towered by disappointment
An honour of personal goals
It's been an hour now
Saw conjuring behind a towel
Never admitted but open deducement
Reversing to find out how
Nobody else is doing this
Exact frame of mental ability
Direct until overfill
Barrel next to current filled
Avoid iconic of all
To be in front when barrels explode
It's been a week already
Never practiced what deconstructed
Her eyes were hard to concentrate
Yet heart of what tasked purposes
To have it done to prevent wrongdoing
Awareness of her suffering gone

It's been however it's now
With heart in voice
Now attempt vocal sounds.

17. OH THE PLACES YOU'LL GO

Oh the places you'll go
Once taught first of choice
Ongoing into a routine
Organised until speaking up
Openly flouting of their desires
Out marched fingers touched
Oil blood money left in charge
Oligarchs programmed not important
Only personal lives mattered
Oh the places you'll go
Once heard a thousand "No's"
Ongoing case of misunderstanding
Organised defence complete bare skull
Openly breaking hearts confirming prejudice
Outright spark in conscience and hearts
Oil burns from charitable not exploit
Oligarchs are getting away with their plot
Only noticed if looked to find stuff
Oh the places you'll go
Once you come to acceptance
Ongoing means they will look to kill you
Organised crimes a different level dimension
Openly same difference as must be presumed
Out the Hotel after dark taxied

Oil from running yet no blood
Oligarchs in a building shouted towards
Only noticeable when unknown it was more fun
Oh the places you'll go once defensives installed
Once upon a time disgusting protocol ongoing
Spoke up and they organised to stop my shouting
Oh the places you'll go
And each memory condemned
To be misremembered what said
or how it looked or even went
Every memory interrupted with
"But why didn't you stop the Oligarchs?".

18. BASTARD GOD

What's the point of being God
If you cannot be greatest bastard
Together bring and force apart
Reunite but then kick and twist
Fate's knife deeper
When it all seems a happy dream
Take away from the cruelest seems
Create and destroy too literally
Not that easy appears simplicity
Listen in surveillance
Why if they're powerless
Better weapon is out from their hands
Not just any time and every sight
Well you can but just distance over globe
Enabled through reasoning a circle
Nature limit questioning
Kept further inquiry dizzy
But constant speed
Unfold passing hours made faster
When there's no speech
Find a purpose in creator
Outlining world in perfect order
And the lives who never thought
Hostages or enough to breathe out

Doesn't exist until marked as found mouth
That's a closing argument for opening speech
Of how the point of being God
To anyone can be
Lives in the power of rhymes
And fiction to bring down
The minute your almighty
Has such whims.

19. "HELP!" SCREAMED THE ENVELOPE

There was an envelope in the sand
A paper damsel granules bound
Who can save from tide
The sheet folded intrigue
Until soaked and brittle lifeless
Not able to read or understand
You there! Be that hero!
Grab the paper off the sand
Dust and open not even sealed
Read the note aloud inside
It says, and the wind dropped
To increase the noise of voice
The note reads "You are great idiot!
I should deserve buried into ground
As long attention on and read
My power evolves and increases the dead
Across planet yet unsuspected
Never murdering whoever surrounding
Just those innocents who never heard
Aware had been written down
Sentenced to death buried in sand
Rescued by idiot oblivious!"
Wind changed temperature
Paper and envelope into bin

The family walked home
Switched on the evening news
A headline of death continual
From across the globe at minimum
Reached out into the cosmos
Gloved hand reaching out death
The newspapers didn't arrive
At depots a panic ate stock
The family had breakfast
Keeping quiet it could be the last
In the bin at the shore
Nothing crossed blew overhead
On their highest survival or death
The cobbled stone litter bin
Still repelled the birds and rats
Tide came in slowly as if
Aware of the danger paper
Final resting place to be uncollected
Tide breakers amplify swearing
And endless seemed the raining
Onto the soaked but mission complete
Of the mysterious buried paper trap
Whatever plan oblivious
Whoever designed revenge
Wherever survives curious
Whyever defined intent

On the shoulders of the family
"Because it kept the youngest HAPPY!!!
So not CRYING! For the LETTER!!
Found buried in front of TRICKLE!!!
Of damaging water!
A sweet child...
It felt more natural
Rather than hands of adult
So future generations skip and chant:
'An envelope! Screamed! For! Help!
Lured rescuers into traps!
Condemns the Earth!!
With! It's! Dirty! HANDS!!!'".
IUndoTimeWithMyLoveIUndoTimeWithMyLoveI
UndoTimeWithMyLove
There was an envelop in the sand
Don't touch it.

20. THE CHALICE IN ANOTHER'S HANDS

The chalice could have been mine!
Until relaxed about others in line
More claim procrastination shame
Beside the centre of perfect storm
The fight has rage that's driven back
Further jewels dangled up for sale
The fist rose up from punched
More open to unite
Away from distraction to revolt
Which enables less control
But as one with directed votes
Arrange different seating at table
So when ask now all we could
Yet still need more of blood
As one united say:
"No. That's enough."
Reclaim the message
Keep in safest hands
Once when not for sale
Restoration shows limits
Capable from a public
The enemy got to first
With the stumbling from hungry
Should the chalice fall into hands

Due to outlook of the marked
The fightback a purpose
My hands start
After what they noticed
Their same promise is false
Whatever happens best result
Someone other
From chalice glugged
My part of seeing it happen
On my watch.

21. SKY COMPASS FOR HUMAN COMPOST

The stars were our guide
And that distance of blame
Used by the con industry
Straight down face to face
Inflicted every second
Front door leave
Or Radio broadcasts
Somehow made to a screen
The stars were our guide
But we've since improved
The system used accuracy
Right down to hair
On a desert flea
Thanks for incremental
Radioactive particles
Now everything glows in the dark
And the stars a fantasy art
Grown millionaires of blood money
Inherited fire rockets towards
The stars were our guide
Ask a Sailor but then you'll get back
Why aren't you uniform and badge
Then difficult from subject change extract
Lean against spine extracted past

Validation of the exam results
The stars were our guide
Because in daylight
If they moved they would be killed
A dramatic way of saying nothings changed
Guided to our star of
Satellite broadcasts
Watched in horror
And hoped never allowed
Just kept on ground
Looking up at stars
While millionaires fired rockets
That blew up or crashed down
The stars were our guide
But we've since through directly
Found ways to serve the dark lord
Whilst being told was facing the light.

22. W IN A RING WITH IT'S DIFFERENCES

Without ours
You know it's needed
When introduced to
Has to be in your hands
Walk on that's possible
Distract the memory
Worrying minute eye contact
Disregarded useless secret
With equalship cutting off same
You soon reveal fuse that could explode
Without code
You know it's useless
When engaged heart in throat
Has to be a test or wise stand
World learn next year almost
Yet still be allowed crude party drinks
Wiped out in retaliation
Today just seems it happened
Worse the useful secrets kept
Resistance met encourage Dance instead
Wait until designated favourite script
A circle surrounds talking aloud
Who threw punch negotiate
Told of stay home better sounding

We know exactly what next happens
Motorway planned but still insistent of Jetpacks
Weirdly lie built up forgotten more believed
To focus on partner and constant surrounding
Walk protective rewarding silence
Stretch out the goodbye anything happens
Wonder is the future after never works up
Hope left safer before thoughts paying off
Wedding before the meddling assumed duties
Build life again once escaped the abuses.

23. THE SHINE REVERSES IT'S DECLINE

They regret in the humour
Of second appointment missed
Swollen over edges of limiting
Balance with hearts in electric
The world sold to fool
It was just there for pokes
And curtains in a hand opened
Never exact the scene with fears
Guidelines bent cause of anger
Rolled across when instructed help
Another to categorise until
The shine reverses it's decline and
Deprives rehearses tricks on mind
Time kept remembers licked sunlight
Rewind escape proof hatches blindfolds
And yet remembrance trip in rainfall
In crime run further skip the formal
Last time re-emergence matches widening circle
Unwind renegadeless whipped for top prize
Denied rulings suspect innocent why
So mind restless dosage wish for sky
Put it down rabid bits of crying
Womanhood register stitch undone the lied
Nothing left respectfulness if thought alive
The final retrospective which steps the dying

Regret in the humour
Instant in huge factor
The shine reverses it’s decline
More times water can remember.

24. THEE INSTRUCTED

The instructions are complicated
Usually works as distraction
How many times said
And speed of reply
When known of the signals
No marks for respect
Or answer question divert
Just intention of shut down
Water under the bridge
The instructions are made out
More important once learned
Instructions come from rules
Down into pack of cards
In pocket humanity
Allow itself to reduced to
The instructions are complicated
But chip away with knowledge
Some even find methods
Of arriving working backwards
The memory is kept alive
The anxiety kept screaming
The concentration always own voice
But voicing a cartoon lady
Or felt stop frame animation

Identityless but still trusted
On than vision and theatre of actions
The rulebook never torn up
But egotistical leave their pen marks
So when history takes from protective case
Lettering and words indecipherable
Of vandals with egos preserved
The instructions are complicated
So that it's easier to reduce
Into states of rage and frustration
Taken with inanimate nearest
Smashed against the cardboard
Walls and boxes the allowed
Contained into
All they had to do
Was just complete the first question.

25. VENTRILOQUIST DISEMBODIED

Wasps trained Citizen Kane re-enactment
"Oh you get the laughs but our existence pointless."
Upon locating Executive Producer credit settle hourly
"Once this complete we'll have no purpose."
Do not introduce unless electric current produced
"Of all things written this is how I'll be."
Not to be used as life preserver or weapon
"Still hear screams of children drifting away."
Hopscotch logic twisted lipstick candy
"Well it was nice knowing you, bye."
Do not operate but still remain influenced
"Oh? Last bit? Wait..."
Television repeats of the stung incident
"Swoops up every time polled."
Got back in the box and it turned out to be a field.

26. DAFT MORT

We listened to your letters
Because you listened to our dreams
Now prepare for consequence
Swept off under your feet
Always go to gravity repelled
In your thoughts first mention of name
A bombastic that didn't leave hanging
Just cradled back to Earth
Fragile system of cells
It happened when closed eyes
Trying listening own plan
Only tribute worthy
Translate French
I listened to your signals
Transmission now complete.

27. KisS

A photojournalist in her native land
From snippets of her classroom experience
At the front of the room a portrait
Of the American President
In her class they shouted insults towards
Classroom piano she played the four notes
Of biggest hit from supergroup British
Corrections when hearing racist words
Towards President her spirit's strength
A story determined to unfold
Perhaps her red trousers a symbol?
Post traumatic displacement
When Iron Curtain thought deficient
Begins to show it's corpse
The bodies of her friends
Known as back of hands
Began piling up and influenced
Of planted heroin
Protest bought arrest
It was unclear after that
A chance moment in a city
I got adopted more a stranger
From under feet and on the breeze
Now continuing in Metropolitan largest.

28. WHEN THE MUSIC IS HOPELESS

You know the music aggrieves you
Slightest thing off balances
What intended of peaceful
In an environment built up
Praise acceptance gradual
Apart from the seating arrangements
Sarcasm or honest
A respect towards feelings
It's not much of a white flag
If it hits ground stumbling
Inadequate
The myth they want a good time
The assumption just there for entertain
The reasoning at least one is opening
The applause taking over
But mainly silence
How much concentration fumbles beats
What number of sounds ring truth
Where did Music originate
First question cross referencing
What story told its journey
Can it look into mirrors
Highest light of daytime
Whatever internal how does it surface?

How near is the Prison Boat of friends
Who beside in a lined up gang
And just how deep their belief
In the sounds
But how open to contribution
And what is this meant to prove
Record the broken clock electric
The leads reliance upon being connected
All down to positions of fingers
So where comes the grievance?
Was it keeping another's time
Or disappointment none fall
Down at feet at concentrated
Movements of fingers on strings
Hitting skins or pressing keys
Or has that voice reminded choice
Of a message beyond tones
They sit to absorb sounds
For their intentional talk
And what notes reach faster
Than your language using words?
The myth they came for a good time
Against that desire you should give them more.

29. THROATS AND PILLS IN PSYCHOLOGICAL

Tilt head back
Chocolate throat and medication
Shrug off the vital hours without
Another day of health tomorrow
Repayment not billed yet
Just that one night
In mouth but couldn't swallow
Waste of a fight against blind
Next time beseech a smaller brand
That works it's magic at nighttime
With just one single
Head back tilted on
That night couldn't swallow pill
Has ended.

30. 3,2,1.

Children playing outside
Neighbourhood bond
Sunshine
Last happy scream
Now silence
Rumbling
Heated through glass
Directed at
Sufferer
Rumble of machine
In passing
Location
Another happy day
Don't concentrate
Problems
Now say goodbye
For now
Continuous
Shine obscures view
Thin greying
Blue
Kept touching rhythm
Designed for
Living

End here now
Demonstration powers
Known
Children playing outside
Never knowing
Perpetuity.

31. 5 YEARS FEAR

Crashing without escape route passport
Exploited ashamed insisted remove involvement
Because of this everything linked
Every lie, exaggeration now sticks
Built upon foundation original sin
Get the message about temptation
Yet cannot account explain process
Instructions of proof desired out
Continually but met with response
Not to worry voice soft
As if woman thought controllable
My protestations went on record
This has now ruined everything
What an end to story
I did see the warnings
And I plead more exploited
Mirror to my own vulnerability
Realised lesson of true friendship
Look through window now sinister
Expect the blue light approaching
Feel the air under suspicion
Scroll through messages was insistent
Knew was immoral changed heart
Caught underneath the collapsing pyramid

How beautiful from the air
From now on things different
Own affairs in order now
Contact express wait for judgement
Will labour out from recompense
Lifelong warn of the result
Of desperation and listening to
Wearing mask of a friend
Underestimation of how things work.

32. SELF PORTRAITURE

We asked a complete stranger
To capture the essence
And because no digital mapping
To assist in designing message
Efforts came instead of laughing
No task instruction
Just tool with a subject
Orwellian portrait
To stare directly at you
Do the fumes soothe or talk to
Advice from vapours in light
A portrait comprising of numbers
Stitched onto the papers
From machine bleeding outwards
We aren't monsters we gave silence
The artist entirely surrounded by failures
A judgement of asking public
Not who it's of but can they see
If my self portrait became the subject
Would I paint a mirror distorted
The complete stranger completed portraiture
Now challenged to paint the gun
Into their own face being held
More effort towards evidence of signature

So named victim on museum plaque remembered
For a month ran an exhibition
Of self portraiture of humans
There was a face of numbers
Glare of camera lens
And my own self portrait
Nine times of dead haunted
And in the celebration of something
To Cromwell paid tribute with burning
The gallery engulfed smoke and flames
The self portrait of more things for saying
It's we of all standing remaining
And the painted flakes all kept away
In the locked safe
Inside the private vault
We asked a complete stranger
If they could judge the painted false.

33. 2,4,6,8 WORD EULOGY

My Dad
Taking me from ride
Countdown in the rhythm to catch
Years later still count up in his memory.

34. OXYGEN WENT

The air was still
Could almost be grieving
And every question over matter
Received silence
The less comfortable
Dismissed on sight in anger
But kept white armour shining
The excuses of trying help
But without communication
Due to manipulation in the papers
Willingly paid for in coinage
First assumption in the humans
The air was still and crying
But that was mistaken
It was really still processing
Continuing to play over again
The events leading up to moment
Now the cause had actually fled
We finally had answers
It just took generations
The oxygen cashed in
Before the noises bought forward
Thought all would be complacent
Wouldn't be there for seeing descent

The air never thought of vengeance
Just carried on with it's purpose
The water froze so with telepath
Was able to find out incident
Unsuspecting humanity staggered on
The mountains were next in the chain
Everything mouthless on the same page
The insults of bipeds
Took another holiday
The caves expressed an interest
The air still didn't touch it.

35. MEMORIAL KNOCKOUT

The pain in the back
Of the head to remind
Warn of disappear to fantasy land
Kept apart from the here and now
Although fascinate
Can actually materialise clear
For some seconds actually
See more than breathing
Reality crash on the legs
Head rocking leaning forward
Door opens with strength
Accident with nobody to laugh
Comforting the hot pain into soft
Once rage explains
Head pushed laughing back
So proposal
Holiday foot on ground
In a corner of a room
Deny present location
Go beyond cartoon
Call on vestiges
Doctors warned could still use
Go there
For how long but remember
Knock on head
Increase the safety
Of the arranged
But daylight follows rest
Tomorrow's result
On the spot with no concept
Where is correct thread?

A mark on the back
Of the scalp for sometime
Always funny if another person saw
What dangers
Of just thinking somewhere
When nobody around
And fool whatever listens in.

36. CORPSE IN A SUITCASE

Tiny people in a suitcase
Execution method failsafe
A discovery of too late
With a scent that asks
The wrong questions
Blue Moon or a trademark
Starts up investigation
In no thoughts
Humiliation possible accident
Flight case if stopped running
Blown off legs when enquire
Picnic of doesn't concern
From swam ashore
Seeking boredom
Where highest threat
Walking home or washing up
Circle turn inwards
For simplification
Away from the depth
Known only to head
Asphyxiated in case and left
Discovery after telephone call
Malice so ingrained thought it game
A warning coded to stay in the line
The murder of suffocation
Pages turned put back to mind
Build me a corkboard
Articles cut out use coloured string
Every time a person died
Found encased in a suitcase
Because of reasons still deeply locked.

37. HATE THAT NO YOU DON'T

You don't hate
It's just the memories
At once making sense
Feel attack embarrassment first
Dragged away for too long
Eventually face ground trod on
Blame and praise your association
Was it a game? No
Efforts made from heart
Inside grown until bursting waters
Of your own adventure carried on
Nothing of sides just disguised
Influences reactions from
You should turn down volume
Put the headphones back on
You can't hate
If you can make from it
A map that charts
Whatever claimed progression
To unfurl accuracy needed
A larger room
Personal marks too afraid to
History first taken away
From personal welcome
To your contribution
Help or conquer
Masses or just one
All fortune in time
You are here now
And if currently distracted
Know closer to peace and sense

Of history joking stolen forced back.

38. DUALITY AT LAST

Used beneath a river bridge
Summer day and School finished
Quiet grounds and Sports field
And human trolls beneath smoking
I looked at the underneath
Mused "That's somewhere you could live"
Looked at two sides of the coin
Before I knew it right back home
Bias instead of trampolines
Wires misread not functioning
Healthy living allocated insisted
On suspicion instead of improvement
Selection liars provide Olympics
Training overridden by accusation
Malice bombing many dreams in step
Wellbeing kept advertisements seeing.

39. A PUPPET DANCE DENIED

Appointment intention
Juggled around duties
Now preparation timetable
Sounds of timer continuing
Sun was out but went
Staring up the road
Window for impact
Complete decline
Not feared of spying
But a cancelled bus service
Why incompetence is surrounded by sabotage
Know next time of cruel tricks
And tactically get arranged
So when stood it was noted
Timetable no longer the vulnerable
The road is ghost in daylight pause
Diversion with nobody told
Oldest trick in their panicking book
Resolve switched higher than it rings up
By side intention just anything normal
Underfoot pulled road timetable
Excluded increases their efforts
To keep out for good insurrection
Flicker of their fool's gold
Using power but draining
On every television signal
As if breaking free of control
The defiance of a puppet's dance
Now as write these words
The road now busy
At least up turned.

40. ON THE SURFACE LOOKING DOWN

Yes it's rushing to the surface now
It's noticed... Aware of it
Things left unsaid as ghosts
Arguing over steering wheel
Of conversation and word orders
Where there is calm
It can be kept in pocket
Helps make sure nobody else's
But now surrounded
With plans to awaken
Concrete again became frightened
Hope it's buried away
Under own weight
Below dark waves
Not disturbed at night
But that forgets morning
It's all coming back to the surface now
Autopsy linguistics complete ignorant of
How far can your seat get from blame
At feet intact from surfaced
What mystery solved with purpose
Give the name to it's catalogued
Parts brushed laboratory put
Waiting for the science to answer
So wake one day to a side
Complete society divided
Of how to what surfaced answered
Yes it's all rushing to the surface now
The black dots on white shaped arrowed
Once discovered why do we all look behind?
The surface never appreciated it's kindness.

41. REFLECT THE HOT METAL BACK

The newspaper headlines revealed
It loses favour meant crime revered
Dull who saves her extensions concerned
Above mirror table quick eye observed
Cut booster levels defend line for real
Worried loose traitor prevents lies repealed
Inert cruise missiles beside unsealed
Worst proves later check signs reneged
Spot true saviour against time relayed
Enough nude hatred pastimes relations
Rough tuned stapled into mind remembered
Stuck immune factor bled dying restored
Stop doing metered bedtimes revision
What improved makers bred fine revulsions.

42. SPRING HAIKUS

Outside of the plan
Warm bright despite circumstance
New cycle behind
Consistent weather lies
Awake in the foraging
Ice's dealt hands dead
Once savings upon
It lessens desires and then
To another watched
Sunlight of your dreams
Until the daily knead
One last kiss of rain.

43. MISFIRE KENNING

Beat moments hide with a breath in
Chop short
No further
Be damned
Peace
Horror
Harmony
Overridden
Record
Results from
Not lost find one word
You've lost it
Laughed I hadn't
Horrifically harming
Betraying servicing
Sorrowful saying
Honouring attentive
Raping repulsions
Heaviest heartbreak
Why did the men untouched
Gathering intended tribute
Has to be addressed
From horror comes peace
Nothing can override harmony
A pulse alive
The loss cannot be of everyday.

44. DYING PEN, CONSTANT HOWL

Buzz of the eardrum hearing nothing
Traffic none still detecting echo
Glad to feared insubtantiated put
As if hearing tuned directly
From the echoing from the heart
Cutting through washing constant
A pounding rhythm performed
Cymbal metal sharper humming
Violent strokes can be noted
Desires known to move any further
One day wake up everything's meaningless
One day wake up happier mood
One day wake up and it's all changed
No longer a buzz in the ear
More the wind inside the skull
As if picked from the shore
One night through sand out crawl
One night found vacant and starved
One night it turned back around
Confession
Did you mean to write of the skull?
Answer
No, Interrogator, the intentions of soul
Question
Did you mean to go along with plot?
Replied
Idiocy only understand
Objection clearly strung along
Lost thread lost what are saying
Lost concentration lost in fiendish
calculate

Telling my friend the buzz of the eardrum
Who is telling me got it wrong
The noise described echo
Blocked whistling direct level
It's the sound that is the importance
Operating the limbs, body and walking
The noise in the ear wants to see the world
And constantly screams out the rage at preventing
Buzz of the eardrum those established high pitched
No music or visual flick speechless but in breath
The drones and rings escape
What speeches do they make
In the dreaming
One day another thing done
One night was all it took
Confession
Misunderstood question
Listened to answer
But preferred the howling
Beside the hearing.

45. THE APOCALYPSE CIRCUIT HAS A NEW TURN

Open Mic location flyer printed off
Stared in hand one more time
On her back walked instrument
The wind blew away the warm
Of the sunshine's finale
And the dirty walls mocked historical
Extension of limited time before rock-fall
There doesn't appear to be customers
And where are the cars parked?
Look through a window and future
Imagines how it could start
Not stepping another foot towards
Instinctual from survival course
But then a shadow from inside
Walking past a light source
Maybe they have further scores
The strap against her breast
Pulled across tightly on her shoulders
She was getting hungrier
The broken sign advertised service
In her mind when glanced at fire escape
Would make a great location
She mutters
"We all have to start from somewhere
What better welcome
than an end of a world?".

46. VALIALAND CONTAINS SKILLS RESULTING AMUSEMENT

Valialand in history a victim nation
But then walls pulled down towards freedom
To keep people in vital half place
Talent Shows broadcasting live made
Disparity of those without TV kept quiet
Welcome the next act, a couple human beings
Act purported to be;
"Tobacco Troll Twins!"
Noise and cued in music
Lucky viewers only hear
Before their act performers explained
"My name is Handrell!
And Georgie is my friend!
We go back a long
To under river bridge
There we learned to sing to smile
Allow us to perform our act right now!"
The young acting took off their blankets
Cameras directly golden television moment
The audience fascinated overpowered in emotion
For the old...
...a choking thought of never saw again
For the young...
...unfair high that in life condemned to chase
After the act televised decompression
Gratitude, inspirations and ultimate message
"I want money, cars! People Army!"
But Handrell disagreed with Georgie
"No! I want to help entire world!
Especially the war orphan boys and girls!"

Audience heartwarming results coming in
Handrell and Georgie qualify next round!
Dressing room alone next episode Georgie
Really wants to break up act shortly
Handrell excluded from discussion
Corner of room came another man
"Georgie is the real star! Signed contract!
Georgie will inspire propaganda monster!"
Handrell didn't cry when explained
The success if gone separate ways
Contestant forfeit!!!
Handrell walks alone back home
In Valialand you were still able to
The limousine driving to airport
Manager asked Georgie to sing that song
It sounds different? And Not.Good.
But we can tell you what to sing of
Under the bridge sobbing Handrell is
Echoes and memories absorbing
Then rage at the ideas stolen
Until large from a dimension
And walking beside them...
Helicopter altitude Georgie nostalgia fooled
Insists one final sweep over bridge
When door ripped off by arm of Troll
Inside the vehicle crushing skulls
On ground Handrell watched unfold
That's why into their blanket carried
Anonymity prize reflecting what lies
Stones and insults directed towards
In Valialand, the rivers drained
Bridges dismantled soil filled in
Still in Valialand half place bought construction

On radio in canteen of such building
Modern cover of the act repeating
That broke in two because easily
Rage at betrayal summoned a Troll
Avenging pipedream open soul
And now walks surviving, Handrell
In their blanket withholding own thoughts.

47. AGAIN WITH FEELING

It was a feeling that I'd never had before
Answered question what you'd do when involved
Demands for explanations of how
To describe uncharted feelings
At the exact spot and time
With no regard the feelings come
During fleeing or fighting whatever happened
It was a feeling that I wished to have before
No words just feelings backed up by force
Except it would still glass shatter
At my feet and down from shoulders
How it always kept noticing
The uniqueness of my outlook
Incompatible with battles fought
It was deceiving wearing joke moustache
It was easily I'd never had before
It's through reading that I learned of how it falls
It was breeding and happy in clinic by walls
It was a meaning categorised until withdrawn
Own voice escaped dissection worse
Left to bang against their glass
Took apart by self inspired mirrored
Limitations over crosswords
But opening the wavelengths
Of diamond grounded kinship.

48. WHO INSTEAD OF HOW

It was an unfamiliar place
Where concern being watched
Actually noticeless at start
Only when attention drawn
Every other time left alone
No idea of thinking or their story
Current dilemmas and longer term goals
Everybody just pretended to be someone else
Until directly spoken to
When left to devices half split
Task in hand and desert island
Man walks into a bar
The premises turned into shop
Hardest buying largest chocolate bars
Woman buys a Scooter toy
Nobody asks her where is child
And there is laughter now using hoverboards
Unfamiliar another language as French
Writing out Income Tax returns
And other fines just being in time occurred
Unfamiliar never had thrown out from aeroplane
Unfamiliar bottom with oxygen on beach surface
Unfamiliar one day there in her kitchen
When the noises began happening
Shouting followed by explosions
Glass breakages and weaponage
Previously unaware and first thought Alien
But it wasn't instead the unfamiliar
Have to flee a refugee survivor
What exact hit with
Revealed a day later

They were tasked with Ambulance
Intensive exact training
It became unfamiliar territory
Until so more than cards
Shuffled into herded pack
But of actual means
And identity failings
To reverse damage
Centuries hangover
The unfamiliar future
Currently finding us
Clinging to.

49. "NOTICELESS" AND THE RED LINE

Noticeless accepted
But not description
Of rocks falling
What other uses got unlock
Stands to reason if past
And present along with personal
Ownership perspectives
The world makes sure
You usually only know
Three
But applied to every word
The containment fulfilled
So opposite nothing of crops
Language chased this down to "Less"
Other cultures mastered first
Forceful always gets made joke
And never look straight eyed again
"What three perspectives?..."
You, me and they hereafter
An Empire is only as strong
As it withstands the light of day
And without the microchip
What could have done?
Insisting a real word
"Noticeless" could reason
It just seemed odd
The microchip thought rocks
Had never in their life
Be of use or ability
Could drop from above
Elevated height or sky

Noticeless has best trick
It only mocks you
Upon noticing this
Noticeless
Face sentence
To have name stretched
Into worsened logic
Noticeless recidivist's particulars made of sprint
Ministers but of worse learn who friend
Better fixed blowing kiss motionless stop doing this
Protest tease marching feet atrocity lists benefits
Current address Budapest Universe another trick
Hoarding grip Hotel wing motorboats draining curse
Brittle mess no it's test chrysalis owning this
Prognosis if feel tricked hosting it don't feel kicked
So anyway noticeless
Accepted correct biologic machinery
Yet rocks falling as one word
The microchip rejects the spelling
But what sort of answer
Too much time on hand?
There are now two states
Observing draining and rare
And the carefree
Noticeless
Will it open door?
Noticeless knows you
Know of it
So
Keep going until forgotten

It’s only the best plan
Until they start giving orders
How far does the charade of following
In the hopes they all becomes noticeless.

50. YOU READ BECAUSE AFRAID

Straightforward nothing at sides
Overlooked majority in fear
Burned with so many offers
And noises on brink of distortion
The colours ongoing until throbbing
So much hurt and comfort seeking
Anything less cast aside weeping
Last chance you want straightforward
I can gently hold you over the chaos
Watch the unstuck on a loop reversed
And back to time when reading words
I'll be straightforward
Aware of relaxant
But without pills or injections
A straightforward consciousness
Cast against the universe for jests
To distract from nothing happens
Without adverts
Intention to give extra
Pull from out space time and physic
So perhaps comrade of true privilege
Too look watching ink for it to sink in
Dealing with the straightforward of frightened
Even more straightforward
Could bring to your Earth the right words
That keeps you sharpened
Protected negate harmful
Straightforward asked
Is this right to limit question
To one straight answer
For so lost words and entertainment

Straightforward back imagination lack
My cocoons damage proof
Except for violence
Of another sale lost
There was a blink
Don't know what happened
But now suddenly all words
Are suspect
Conditioned assessed
What could have been
Five lines of joke
Knifed in the back at your own birthday party
All friends and relation attending with special guest
A head of electronics with daggers in a cage
The chorus of wishes for birthday all being sung
Candles of symbolism atop cake flames
And on the "Dear-" blade into ear
Last hear your name if was a scream
That grip of life and the pain
To focus on nothing else
Did assailant escape where others killed?
What is current temperature of day
Straightforwardly that's pitch
Can take you away but straightforwardness
Because forgotten numbers one to several
If can read then can assess frightened
If frightened desire increase of calm peace
If peace is calm then invisible mountains
If mountains invisible poor traffic control
If traffic controlled expect all on wheels
If wheels then either spinning or inert
It's that straightforward.

51. MARKET REASONING

If can read then can assess frightened
If frightened desire increase of calm peace
If peace is calm then invisible mountains
If mountains invisible poor traffic control
If traffic controlled expect all on wheels
If wheels then either spinning or inert
If movement then from source of energy
If energy then civilisation's last gasp
If gasping then a stand back except
If there's exploit that's money slid under desks
If desks then either banged or fallen asleep on
If sleep then hours against civilised and growth
If there's growth it won't be shared right down
If there's down then also sides and the up
If up how timed a day before sunsets
If sunsets how beautiful who you share with
If shared with nobody how treasured secret
If secretive what if told was really straightforward
If straightforward enough then feeling less
frightened
If less then steps press against feet across
If there's across then it caused underneath
If there's underneath it caused stories you'd read
If reading in obvious the capable day
If day then able to get home before sunset
If sunset we've read the instructions
If left instructions maybe become less afraid.

52. BOAT YACHT SHIP TANKER

"We have to remember the people who own the boat"
And right first there
Control attempt of words
Before the argument of passenger
Levels of complicit
What purpose first designed
We have to also never forget
How long the road kicked to pass
In attempt to appease, diminish
Counter accuse then change subject
We have to remember the people who own the boat
How they just left it outside!
Rust and light
Petroleum left to right
Laughed at by Schoolchildren
On transport and then ignored
We have to remember the boat owners
It would be a push
In current vehicle maintenance
A longer excursion detectable
But the boat on the front path
And the power of transitive algebra
Means a child walking past house
Is far closer to international waters
Than his parents feared
Or the child themselves could dream
We have to remember the people who own the boat
But only to diminish the blame of responsibility.

53. UP STEP

The steps with purpose out from shot
None fall all ignore being stared
Just shadows as guides
Step up the white
All facing intention hypnotised
None help all think most of all self
Raceless just a prize to climb
Safe from conditioning
Nothing of life to remind
No signs of women or children
No evidence of left out destitution
No features reaching distinctive
Just outfits standing out matching
Cubes assembled future claims is prison
Alongside collected steps to walk up
To whatever mission
At first glance hallucinated
Through focus
A joke that somebody
Had fallen
To will any excitement.

54. BULLETPROOF GUIDANCE

Yes, the will of touching wood
Connection weakest all unfolds
Builds up other lies
And covert spies
Perfecting ruthless war depots
Yes, the clutching of strings
With shapes to feel things
Bow of covered head
Before prayers kneeling mat
Yes, all that and I do this instead
Don't let me stop you building defence
If enemy is all surround
Than occupied mind
Already confound
Yes, the screaming internal voice
Female octave diction menace
Clarification of saying
The accusations of lying
One last example of lighting
Determination on the paper
To create proof not a traitor
Yes, will see to continuation
Learn not to rueful over
Everybody ignoring trail
Digits miniscule vibrates
Yes, the dust from galactic explosion
With the future irradiation
Forced together with flesh vulnerable
Practical set chosen
Yes these words my bulletproof guidance.

55. "WHO ARE YOU TO TELL ME?"

Well everything is a contest
Self appointed town sheriff
The world and potential
Available constant
So they stand at the gate
Preventing some crossing
"Do you have initials after name?"
Green lit Emperor with paper
In case it hasn't been noticed
The chessboard knocked off table
Chess pieces turning in slow motion
Reversal of roles purpose and function
And still the lies
"While the world is still in flux"
But that's always the result
Into flesh tent poles
And planning granted
For the convulsing
Told it's their fault
Everybody has a story
They land on either side
So trust issues damaged
And that revealed apparent
How they didn't need
Temperature increase
To remain inside
The frying pan
Whoever they are
Notice they need a mob?
To back up why nails
Should always be smashed down.

56. RAINBOW'S END

The rainbow has come to an end
Disbelief of riding clouds
If ever found potted gold
From public knowledge phased out

1. How far did the rainbow last?
2. How long did anybody stare?
3. How quickly was it co-opted?
4. How ruthless was it marketed?
5. How distressing it's relinquish?
6. How obvious did it seem one step?
7. How covered by raincloud spite?

Look who swam back! Good creature
Ask it, "What found out?"

1. The rainbow was far enough to lose companionship
2. Those who did eventually pulled back to hostage
3. The market response was gathered in secret
4. The guilty became innocent when they were first
5. They seemed calmer just internalised
6. The lack of height biggest clue of love
7. Thunder only rained further out from reach

Good creature! Now still believe you
But continual! So other creatures! Set OUT
"Important to let starving without update
Instead of what gets on their plate!"
The creatures swam back onto beach
The rainbow had no registered beginning.

57. THE LANDOWNER WHO HELD OUT TOO LONG

You watched it now
Then read it's newspaper
Everything ran away from
Sooner than destined
Railway station
Timetable given breathing window
Speed of disinterested
Courtesy left to disintegrate
You thought it finished
Dismissed into your past
All time watching taking in
So it was a field
How could there be a wood?
Suggesting land had been stripped away
Shows black holes geographic knowledge
A natural flat plain
Nothing said about lifeless
Always forget in another's hands
Reward tortured kept enclosed
In blocks going upwards
In the distance of land
Everything can be sold
But one final Vampire blood
From the air see coming nearer
The faces needing homes on land
How to make the World better
Make continuing products
For playing in tower blocks
That can see in distance
Below helicopter skids

Interrupting the signals
That had nothing else to grip
The land owner
Who held out too long
Always knew outcome was stolen.

58. INK DEFIES EXTINCTION

It came down to acceptance
That desire to question
Plateau thought indomitable
Was actually just the first page
Nobody asks the questions
That even you don't ask yourself
It's not the obvious "What about it?'
But the more personal of why
The process in two steps
Recognition gone as far
Not even that just want sparks
After dulled themselves into corner
Unknowingly in retreat
The other step is evidence
Notice it does one thing
How can it change
To something else?
Pursuit until intersection
The deal made before enrolment
Aware how ink defies extinction
To write against the indoctrination
And for it to never be saw
By another pair of eyes
Apart from yours
It drives into hand from desk
The steelworks of words closedown
But through night kept running
From expected raining
To emerge hardened
So it's less of problem
Knowing what is saying

The acceptance most of them
Care less
The shrug as it doesn't
Involve them
The cut if false lead
Continues pestering
The lead attempted warm
Of the next contestant.

59. AND SEEING THAT

Now look at them hard
Reach how did it get there
A war of total Mars
Aligned with cause
Reflecting light too brightly
Bowing head gets away once
Expecting other tricks
Given the chance
Rest the eyes
Until it smiles again
Grinning Think
Not as scary just choice
Looked at daylight
Rubbed eyes
Hardly look at them now.

60. SPOTLESS

Spotless passive aggressive
Codeword implication
Nuance emphasis
Order from panicking
And I had to be arguing
Constitution of stains?
Attempted scrubbed clean.

61. WHY ARE THEY BEING FOUND ALONE?

The screaming downwards at
Shadows of nothing bottom stair
All part of the fun
Of watching sunlight dim
Who could be shared with?
Then it comes down to intention
The love rejected if not
Hands and in pieces crushed
Never dared to even think of
There are circumstances
But know could have worse
Discovered alone just secretive corpse
Happens again when thought all in control
Did they hear the laughter of company?
In the noise can't detect own dialect
Does it still echo of their classrooms?
When it didn't hurt for ambitions
With the protection of the adult
Spent the following years figuring out
That could be one reason
And before shouted down the wisdom
Of punishable death for assumption
Why are they being found alone?
What have they done or become?
What failings span age range
Where could they have fitted into?
When blamed for over half they didn't do?
Whatever value of discipline beaten through?
When is the choice of nothing due?
What does it say about where going to?
Where do endings make a room?

62. KHMER ROUGE

Reminiscing
Great lost pastime
First time heard word
Of the massacre's frontline
Atrocity details lost in ringing
Between ears of personally
Getting subject name wrong
Instead of facing
The horrors on people done.

1. FOR SEX WE ARE BLOWN INTO AIR

To spread and continue genetics
Onto a story allegory of perfection
"See how on breeze...
In complete freedom...
Dandelion seeds...
Blow away to a new story...
Or get trapped inside
rusting bucket!!
Be in peril of rising
cigarette's finished!!
This has caused enormous
Self doubt in the Prophecy
And succumb to being a human
Inside universal chaos!!!"
The genetics claimed
At first test failed
And fertile away scared
Also the programming
Around fell down
Amplifying thoughts
Answering in own voice
Anxiety was a mouth under hand
Angrier filed into compartments
Apathy blown up importance
Artillery of unarmed combatants
Another view rejected now
Angled towards light source
Angelic through delirium
Anticipation reduced to look
For nothing
Any enquiries

Run further upstairs
Away but don't tell gravity or seeds
Amnesty for seeds blown into tins
Antibodies on a stalk
Hold the key.

Printed in Great Britain
by Amazon

79399678R00079